A Guide to
AMERICAN STATES

Massachusetts

THE BAY STATE

MEDIA ENHANCED BOOKS
AV2 BY WEIGL
ADDED VALUE · AUDIO VISUAL

www.av2books.com

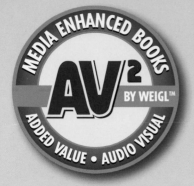

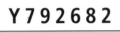

AV[2] provides enriched content that supplements and complements this book. Weigl's AV[2] books strive to create inspired learning and engage young minds in a total learning experience.

Your AV[2] Media Enhanced books come alive with...

Audio
Listen to sections of the book read aloud.

Key Words
Study vocabulary, and complete a matching word activity.

Video
Watch informative video clips.

Quizzes
Test your knowledge.

Embedded Weblinks
Gain additional information for research.

Slide Show
View images and captions, and prepare a presentation.

Go to **www.av2books.com**, and enter this book's unique code.

BOOK CODE

Y792682

Try This!
Complete activities and hands-on experiments.

... and much, much more!

AV[2] by Weigl brings you media enhanced books that support active learning.

Published by AV[2] by Weigl
350 5th Avenue, 59th Floor
New York, NY 10118
Website: www.av2books.com   www.weigl.com

Library of Congress Cataloging-in-Publication Data

Pezzi, Bryan.
 Massachusetts / Bryan Pezzi.
   p. cm. -- (A guide to American states)
 Includes index.
 ISBN 978-1-61690-793-8 (hardcover : alk. paper) -- ISBN 978-1-61690-469-2 (online)
 1. Massachusetts--Juvenile literature. I. Title.
 F73.33.P495 2011
 974.4--dc23
                          2011018333

Printed in the United States of America in North Mankato, Minnesota

052011
WEP180511

Project Coordinator Jordan McGill
Art Director Terry Paulhus

Photo Credits
Every reasonable effort has been made to trace ownership and to obtain permission to reprint copyright material. The publishers would be pleased to have any errors or omissions brought to their attention so that they may be corrected in subsequent printings.

Weigl acknowledges Getty Images as its primary image supplier for this title.

Contents

Massachusetts landscapes include mountains, a river valley, seashores, and farmland.

Introduction

Though Massachusetts is a small state, it has a rich history and is **diverse** in both its landscape and its people. Massachusetts is where 102 Pilgrims landed in 1620 and developed the first permanent European **colony** in what became New England in the United States. Later, many Bay Staters, as residents of Massachusetts are now called, including Benjamin Franklin and Samuel Adams, were leaders of **revolutionary** activity leading up to America's war for independence. In 1773 Massachusetts was the site of the Boston Tea Party, in which colonists protested British taxes on tea by throwing hundreds of chests of tea into Boston Harbor. In 1775 the first battles of the American Revolution were fought at Lexington and Concord.

The Old State House is the oldest surviving public building in Boston. Built in 1713, it housed early government offices.

The first settlers of Plymouth, Massachusetts, were Pilgrims. They arrived from England in 1620.

For much of the 1780s Massachusetts and the rest of the country were governed by a **constitution** called the Articles of Confederation. The government created by the Articles, however, was weak and mostly ineffective. In western Massachusetts in 1786 Daniel Shays, an army captain during the American Revolution, led a protest against high taxes and other economic problems of the emerging nation. The event, known as Shays's Rebellion, was one of several disturbances in different states that helped convince Americans that it was time to create a stronger government. Soon the Articles were replaced by the U.S. Constitution, which Massachusetts formally approved on February 6, 1788. Residents of the state played a vital role in building the new country. John Adams, a Massachusetts native, was the country's second president; John Quincy Adams, his son, was the sixth president.

Where Is Massachusetts?

Massachusetts is part of an area of the northeastern United States known as New England, which consists of six states near the Atlantic coast. The other New England states are Vermont, New Hampshire, Connecticut, Rhode Island, and Maine, the sole New England state with which Massachusetts does not share a border.

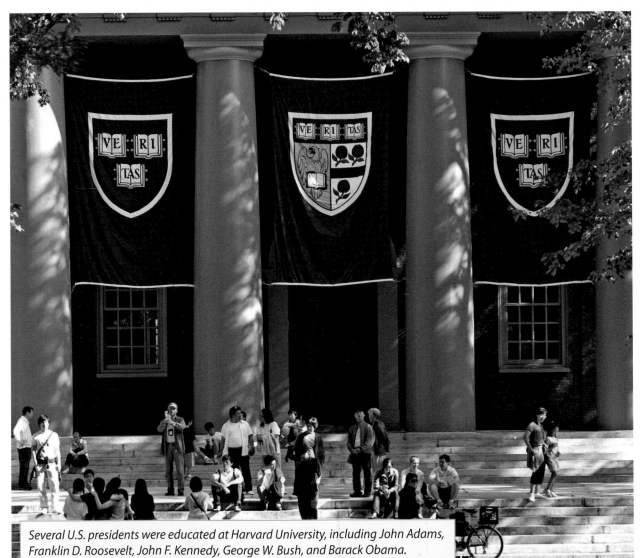

Several U.S. presidents were educated at Harvard University, including John Adams, Franklin D. Roosevelt, John F. Kennedy, George W. Bush, and Barack Obama.

A thriving center of education, culture, and industry throughout its long history, Massachusetts offers both residents and visitors alike a mix of the traditional and the modern. In Boston, for example, a modern skyline exists alongside narrow streets that are hundreds of years old. In Cambridge, students walk the grounds of Harvard, the country's oldest university.

Boston, the state capital, is a transportation hub for New England. Logan International Airport, which is just a few miles from downtown Boston, is among the country's most important domestic and international gateways. The airport has its own fire and police departments, a power plant, and 27 acres of landscaping. Several interstate highways and passenger railroads pass through the state.

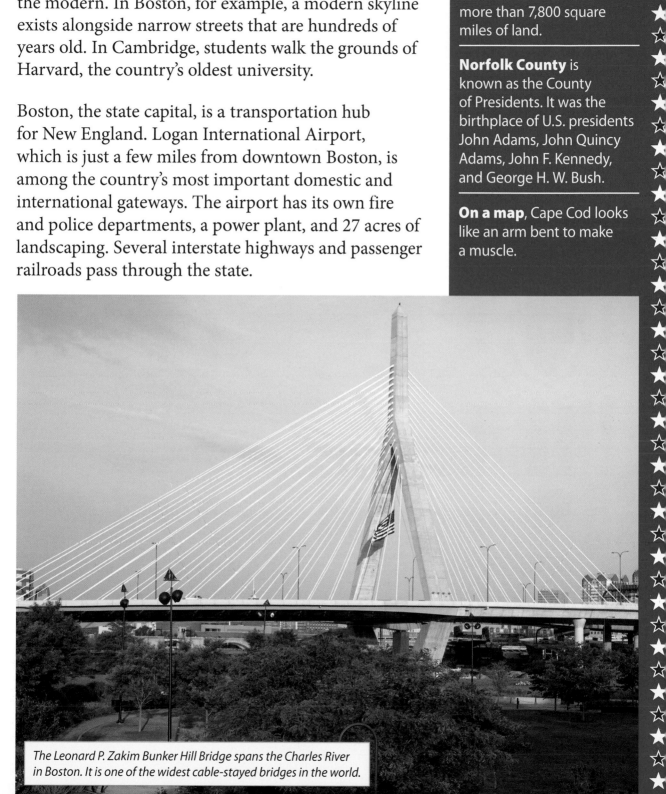

The Leonard P. Zakim Bunker Hill Bridge spans the Charles River in Boston. It is one of the widest cable-stayed bridges in the world.

Mapping Massachusetts

Massachusetts is bordered by the Atlantic Ocean to the east. The New England states of New Hampshire and Vermont lie to the north, and Connecticut and Rhode Island are to the south. Massachusetts borders New York to the west. The state has about 4,200 miles of rivers and more than 1,100 lakes and ponds.

Sites and Symbols

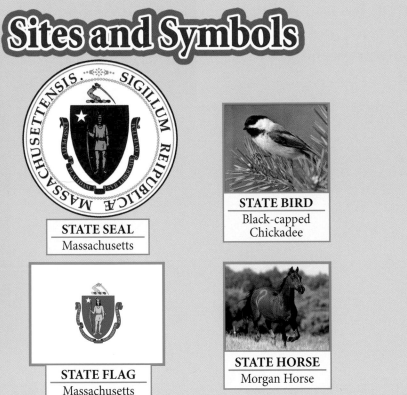

STATE SEAL
Massachusetts

STATE BIRD
Black-capped Chickadee

STATE FLOWER
Mayflower

STATE FLAG
Massachusetts

STATE HORSE
Morgan Horse

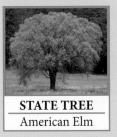

STATE TREE
American Elm

Nickname The Bay State

Motto *Ense Petit Placidam Sub Libertate Quietem* (By the Sword We Seek Peace, but Peace Only Under Liberty)

Song "All Hail to Massachusetts," words and music by Arthur J. Marsh

Entered the Union February 6, 1788, as the 6th state

Capital Boston

Population (2010 Census) 6,547,629 Ranked 14th state

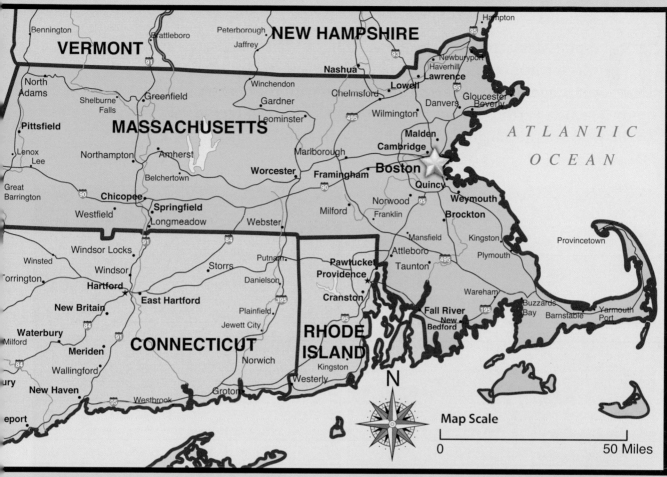

Bennington	
VERMONT	Peterborough · Jaffrey · NEW HAMPSHIRE
	Hampton
	Brattleboro
	Nashua
North Adams	Winchendon · Lawrence
	Chelmsford · Lowell
Greenfield	Gardner
Shelburne Falls	Danvers · Gloucester Beverly
Pittsfield	MASSACHUSETTS · Leominster · Wilmington
	Malden
Lenox Lee	Northampton · Amherst · Marlborough · Cambridge · ATLANTIC OCEAN
	Boston
Great Barrington	Belchertown · Worcester · Framingham · Quincy
Chicopee	Norwood · Weymouth
Westfield	Springfield · Milford · Franklin · Brockton
	Longmeadow · Webster · Mansfield
Windsor Locks	Attleboro · Kingston · Provincetown
Winsted	Storrs · Putnam · Plymouth
Torrington	Windsor · Pawtucket · Taunton
Hartford	Danielson · Providence · Wareham
New Britain	East Hartford · Cranston · Fall River · Buzzards Bay · Barnstable · Yarmouth Port
Waterbury	Plainfield · New Bedford
Milford	Jewett City · RHODE ISLAND
Meriden	CONNECTICUT · Kingston
Wallingford	Norwich · Westerly
New Haven	Groton
eport	Westbrook

N

Map Scale

0 ————————— 50 Miles

STATE CAPITAL

The capital of Massachusetts is Boston. Located on Massachusetts Bay, Boston was settled in 1630 and became the capital of Massachusetts Bay Colony in 1632. Today, about 645,000 people live in Boston, which is the state's largest city.

LEGEND

— Road
— River
⭐ State Capital
• City
▦ Massachusetts
— State Border

United States

Hawai'i   Alaska

Massachusetts

The Land

Despite Massachusetts' small area, it has a varied landscape that was formed by the movement of glaciers many thousands of years ago. In the east is a coastal plain with rocky shores and sandy beaches. Farther inland there are rolling hills and **fertile** valleys. To the west are the Taconic Mountains, the Berkshire Hills, and the Hoosac Range.

MOUNT GREYLOCK

Mount Greylock in the Taconic Mountains is the highest point in Massachusetts. It is 3,491 feet high.

CAPE COD

Cape Cod is a sandy peninsula of glacial origin. It is made up of moraine, the earth and stone that a glacier leaves behind when the ice melts.

CONNECTICUT RIVER VALLEY

The Connecticut River flows from north to south for 66 miles through Massachusetts. Various crops grow in its fertile valley.

BERKSHIRE HILLS

Many peaks in the Berkshire Hills rise to heights of more than 2,000 feet. These hills are part of the Appalachian Mountains. In autumn, the foliage turns beautiful colors.

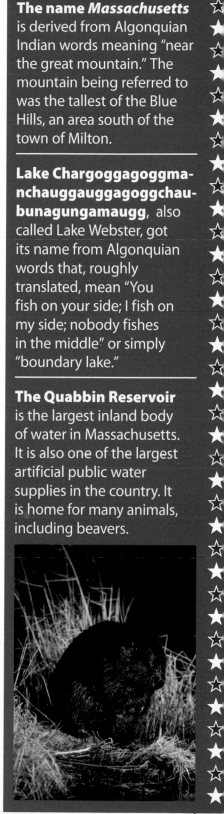

I DIDN'T KNOW THAT!

The name *Massachusetts* is derived from Algonquian Indian words meaning "near the great mountain." The mountain being referred to was the tallest of the Blue Hills, an area south of the town of Milton.

Lake Chargoggagoggma-nchauggauggagoggchau-bunagungamaugg, also called Lake Webster, got its name from Algonquian words that, roughly translated, mean "You fish on your side; I fish on my side; nobody fishes in the middle" or simply "boundary lake."

The Quabbin Reservoir is the largest inland body of water in Massachusetts. It is also one of the largest artificial public water supplies in the country. It is home for many animals, including beavers.

Temperatures in Massachusetts, like the rest of New England, often drop below freezing in the winter.

Climate

Massachusetts experiences hot and cold temperatures during the year but not extremes of either. Coastal regions can get quite hot and humid in the summer. The west is cooler and drier. In the winter, the western and central parts of the state get the most snow, while the Cape gets more moderate accumulations.

The average temperature for the state ranges from 68° Fahrenheit in summer to 27° F in winter. The highest temperature ever recorded in Massachusetts was 107° F in Chester and New Bedford on August 7, 1975. The state's lowest recorded temperature was –35° F in Chester on January 12, 1981.

Average Annual Precipitation Across Massachusetts

Boston, Lowell, Springfield, and Worcester all receive about 42 to 49 inches of rain per year. Some areas receive more than 55 inches of rainfall. Why might some places get more rain than others?

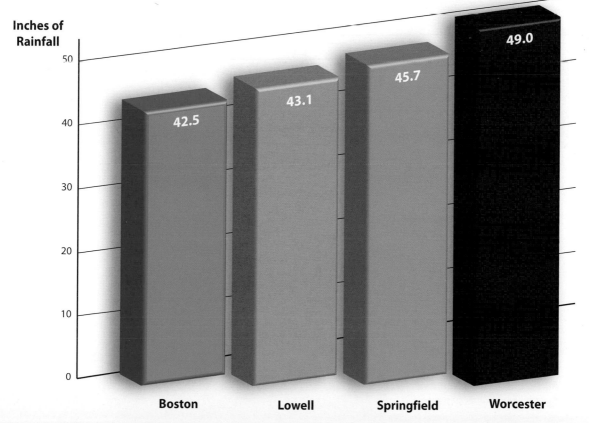

Inches of Rainfall

Boston	Lowell	Springfield	Worcester
42.5	43.1	45.7	49.0

Natural Resources

The Bay State has a long tradition of fishing in its coastal waters. It was the great number of cod that first brought English fishers to the area. **Whaling** was once a major source of income for the state, but the industry declined at the beginning of the 1900s. Cod, however, remains an important catch, along with haddock, flounder, whiting, ocean perch, lobsters, clams, and sea scallops. The Cape Cod towns of Wellfleet and Cotuit are famous for their oysters.

Atlantic cod helped feed the early coastal settlers. This natural resource remains abundant in Massachusetts waters.

Cranberries require acid peat soil, a fresh water supply, and sand to grow. Harvesting takes place in the fall.

I DIDN'T KNOW THAT!

Lobster was not always the delicacy that it is today. Until the late 1800s boatloads of lobsters sold for pennies. Prisoners sometimes rioted at the prospect of another lobster dinner, and a group of servants in Massachusetts won a judgment that they not be served lobster more than three times each week.

Cranberries got their name from Dutch settlers who thought the bushes' flowers resembled cranes.

Clambakes are a New England tradition popular in Massachusetts.

Massachusetts has some mineral deposits. Among those mined are sand, gravel, stone, lime, and clays. Much of the soil in the state is thin and rocky, making it difficult to farm. As a result, agriculture is not central to the state's economy. Milk and eggs are among the most important agricultural products. The cranberry bogs on Cape Cod make Massachusetts a leader in that crop. Cranberries are among the few fruits native to North America.

Plants

Massachusetts has many kinds of plants. Maple, ash, beech, oak, birch, and pine trees are abundant throughout the state. The state tree is the American elm. Adopted in 1941, it commemorates George Washington taking command of the Continental Army under an elm in Massachusetts in 1775.

The Bay State has many kinds of wildflowers. The state flower is the mayflower, which is **endangered**. It grows in the state's woodlands. Other more common wildflowers include mountain laurels, flowering dogwoods, purple giant hyssops, rhododendrons, and violets.

Today more than 100 state forests, reservations, and parks, along with several national wildlife refuges and the Cape Cod National Seashore, provide protection for the state's natural environment. Massachusetts has a history of protecting its natural areas. The oldest public park in the United States is the Boston Common. The 45-acre area was opened as a public space in 1634.

BIRCH TREE

Birch trees have smooth bark with papery layers. American Indians used the bark to build canoes and cover their small round houses called wigwams.

MAPLE TREE

The most important maple tree in Massachusetts is the sugar maple, which is a principal source of maple syrup.

VIOLETS

Wild violets produce brightly colored flowers in the spring. These common New England plants grow best in cool, shady areas.

MOUNTAIN LAURELS

Mountain laurels are bell-shaped flowers that bloom in large white and pink clusters. They are found in many Massachusetts parks.

Animals

Massachusetts has a variety of animals. Few large animals remain in the wild, but bears and moose are sometimes seen in the woods. Other animals of the forest include deer, otters, snowshoe hares, red foxes, woodchucks, and raccoons. The sea supports a variety of fish, shellfish, and marine mammals. Birds include waterbirds such as the loon, land dwellers such as the brown thrasher, and game birds such as the ruffed grouse.

The greatest threat to Massachusetts' animal life is the loss of and damage to the natural **habitat**. Through the years some of the state's species have become endangered or **extinct**. For example, during the time of European settlement, the wild turkey was common. As forests were cut down, the bird disappeared from the area. In recent years, however, it has been reintroduced, and there are now thousands of wild turkeys in the state.

SNOWSHOE HARE

Snowshoe hares change color from brownish or grayish in summer to pure white in winter. They also have heavily furred hind feet.

WILD TURKEY

The state's wild turkey population is about 20,000. A physical trait of the common turkey is a long red piece of flesh called a snood. A snood grows from the turkey's forehead to its bill.

WOODCHUCK

The largest member of the squirrel family is called the woodchuck. Woodchucks are also known as groundhogs. They live in urban and suburban areas of Massachusetts as well as in fields and meadows.

RIGHT WHALE

Right whales are slow-moving mammals that can reach about 45 to 60 feet in length. The species nearly became extinct in the 1700s, and today only about 300 exist. Right whales are protected by law and can be seen off the coast of Massachusetts, particularly near Cape Cod Bay and the Great South Channel.

The state bird, adopted in 1941, is the black-capped chickadee. It is among the most common of all North American birds.

Sperm whales were discovered near Nantucket in 1712, and in the 1800s the area was called the Whaling Capital of the World. Whale blubber was used to produce high-quality oil that could be burned in lamps.

The Boston terrier, recognized as the state dog in 1979, is a cross between an English bulldog and an English terrier. It is one of the few dog breeds native to the United States.

Tourism

Tourism is an important industry for Massachusetts. People from across the country and the world are drawn to the state for its mix of historic attractions and natural wonders. Boston is particularly popular. The heart of Boston is very compact, making it easy to explore on foot. Along the city's Freedom Trail are numerous historic sites. These include Boston Common, the old and new state houses, Faneuil Hall, the Paul Revere House, the Old North Church, and the USS *Constitution*, better known as Old Ironsides. The city contains numerous old town houses and mansions, many of which are situated along the narrow cobblestone streets of Beacon Hill.

Outside Boston, the Massachusetts countryside has many interesting towns, rolling hills, and beautiful hiking trails. On the coast, tourists flock to the seaside and island resorts of Cape Cod, Martha's Vineyard, and Nantucket.

NEW ENGLAND AQUARIUM

Founded in 1969, the New England Aquarium in Boston is a global leader in ocean exploration and marine conservation. Every year more than 1.3 million visitors come to the aquarium to see its African penguins, Atlantic harbor seals, and sea jellies.

MUSEUM OF SCIENCE

Boston's Museum of Science contains several hundred exhibits on astronomy, energy, industry, and natural history.

PLIMOTH PLANTATION

Visitors take a trip back in time to visit Plimoth Plantation. This historic park re-creates the Pilgrims' Plymouth Colony of the 1600s, and it uses the original spelling of Plymouth.

MAYFLOWER II

A copy of the ship that brought 102 pilgrims to Cape Cod Bay in 1620, the *Mayflower II* has sat in the harbor at Plymouth since 1957. It was built in England in the 1950s.

Newbury Street in the Back Bay area of Boston is an elegant shopping district full of galleries, antique stores, and clothing boutiques.

The Naismith Memorial Basketball Hall of Fame is located in Springfield, the city where James Naismith invented the game in 1891. The baskets were originally peach baskets, and the ball had to be taken out every time someone scored.

The original Museum of Fine Arts in Boston opened to the public on July 4, 1876. November 2010 marked the opening of The New MFA, which has a new wing for Art of the Americas.

Industry

Massachusetts was one of the country's first **industrialized** states. The first saltworks and ironworks date back to the 1640s. In the 1800s and the first half of the 1900s the state was known for manufacturing industries such as **textile** production. Some traditional industries, such as textiles and whaling, have since died out. However, the state is still known for its watches, cutlery, guns, and leather goods.

Industries in Massachusetts
Value of Goods and Services in Millions of Dollars

Manufacturing remains important in Massachusetts, but today the largest sector of the economy is service industries. In these industries, workers help or provide a service for other people. What service industries are especially important to meet the needs of the many tourists who visit the state?

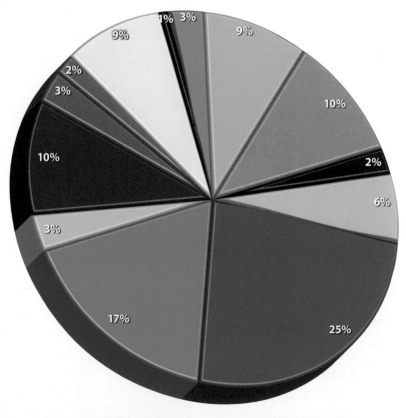

LEGEND

*	Agriculture, Forestry, and Fishing	$800
*	Mining	$152
■	Utilities	$5,321
■	Construction	$12,295
■	Manufacturing	$32,423
■	Wholesale and Retail Trade	$35,721
■	Transportation	$5,647
■	Media and Entertainment	$20,491
■	Finance, Insurance, and Real Estate	$93,084
■	Professional and Technical Services	$60,969
■	Education	$10,086
■	Health Care	$35,690
■	Hotels and Restaurants	$9,893
■	Other Services	$8,816
■	Government	$33,794

TOTAL $365,182

*Less than 1%. Percentages do not add to 100 because of rounding.

Modern manufacturing industries in Massachusetts produce such goods as industrial machinery, electronic equipment, medical supplies, and computer components. Today, however, the state's economy is based largely on technological research and development and on service industries. Many of the state's high-technology companies are based in or around Boston, where there are several leading universities and research centers. The area around Route 128, which circles Boston, has been called America's Technology Highway.

Many historians consider Lowell to be the birthplace of the Industrial Revolution in the United States. In 1823 a cotton mill was opened in the town. The area where the first mills were built is now a national historical park.

Crane and Company in Dalton has produced most of the paper for U.S. currency since 1879.

Boston built a practical subway line in 1897. It was 1.5 miles long.

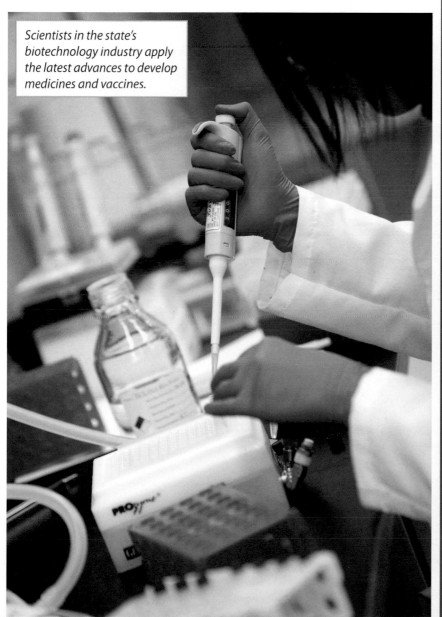

Scientists in the state's biotechnology industry apply the latest advances to develop medicines and vaccines.

Goods and Services

From early in its history, Massachusetts has had a cutting-edge economy. This is especially true of the transportation industry. Brockton had the country's first electric street railway and was also among the first cities to adopt electric street lighting. Boston had the first passenger subway system in the United States. Massachusetts also built the country's first railroad. Today the state has a far-reaching network of highways and railroads. Boston has always been a major seaport for the New England region. Logan International Airport serves as the state's major air transport center.

On a typical weekday more than 1 million riders travel on Boston's mass transit system.

Massachusetts is famous for its excellent colleges and universities. Harvard University, in Cambridge, was founded in 1636 and is the oldest university in the United States. It has educated several U.S. presidents and dozens of **Nobel laureates**. Two other well-known institutions are the Massachusetts Institute of Technology, located in Cambridge, famous for its scientific training and research, and Tufts University in Medford. The state also is home to several of the nation's best women's colleges, including Wellesley College in Wellesley. The University of Massachusetts is the main state-supported school. It has campuses in Amherst, Boston, Lowell, and Dartmouth and a medical school in Worcester.

Researchers at the Massachusetts Institute of Technology are working on improving clean energy. Increasing clean energy use is a goal of the administration of President Barack Obama.

Harvard College, now university, was founded in Cambridge in 1636, just 16 years after the arrival of the Pilgrims at Plymouth.

The Boston Latin School, originally named the Latin Grammar School, was founded in 1635 and was the first public secondary school in the nation. It was open to all boys regardless of social class, setting a standard for tax-supported public education.

The first American newspaper was published in Boston on September 25, 1690. It was called *Publick Occurrences: Both Forreign and Domestick.*

In 1876 Alexander Graham Bell invented the telephone in Boston.

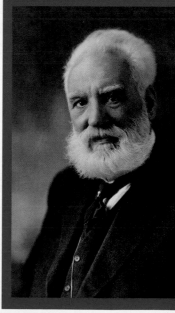

American Indians

American Indians lived on the land that became Massachusetts long before European settlement. Archaeological evidence suggests that they resided in the area more than 10,000 years ago. They developed the land, growing corn, beans, squash, and other vegetables, and also hunted and fished. At the time of European contact, around the year 1500, as many as 30,000 American Indians lived in the area. Most of them belonged to Algonquian groups that spoke related languages.

In 1616 and 1617 thousands of American Indians died from diseases brought by the early European visitors. By 1620 the American Indian population had dropped dramatically, by as much as 90 percent according to some estimates. When the Pilgrims came to Massachusetts in that year, they received help from the Wampanoag tribe. The tribe traded goods with the Pilgrims and shared their techniques of planting, fishing, and cooking.

American Indians, led by Wampanoag chief King Philip, and colonists battled in 1675. The conflict was called King Philip's War.

After the death of Wampanoag chief Massasoit, relations between American Indians and the new waves of European settlers worsened. These troubles led to King Philip's War in 1675. During the conflict some 600 English settlers and 3,000 American Indians lost their lives, and many tribes were wiped out completely.

Like many other Indian tribes Wampanoag Indians from Massachusetts attend powwows to preserve and celebrate their heritage.

The peoples of the Algonquian language family include the Massachuset, the Nauset, the Nipmuc, the Pennacook, the Pocumtuc, and the Wampanoag.

Wampanoag chief Massasoit made a peace treaty with the English after their arrival in Plymouth. The peace lasted throughout his life.

In 1653 John Sassamon became the first American Indian to study at Harvard University. He later became a **scribe** and **interpreter** to the Wampanoag chief Metacom, also called King Philip.

English explorer Bartholomew Gosnold visited the shores of what is today Massachusetts in 1602. After naming Cape Cod, he gave his daughter's name to Martha's Vineyard.

Explorers

Europeans sailed near Massachusetts before the arrival of the *Mayflower* at Plymouth in 1620. According to legend, the Northern European explorer Leif Eriksson visited New England in about 1000. In 1497 and 1498 the famous explorer John Cabot sailed along North America's Atlantic coast, and his voyages were the basis of England's claim to the region. In 1602 the English explorer Bartholomew Gosnold explored the peninsula that he named Cape Cod for the cod that were plentiful in the waters.

At this time many Europeans saw New England as a land of possibilities. However, it was not trade or the search for wealth that brought the first permanent settlers to the area. In 1620 a group of Pilgrims arrived in Massachusetts looking for religious freedom.

Timeline of Settlement

Early Exploration

1498 Italian explorer John Cabot, sailing for England, sees North America's Atlantic coast for the first time.

1602 Explorer Bartholomew Gosnold explores the coast of New England and gives Cape Cod its name.

1605–1606 France's Samuel de Champlain draws detailed maps of the New England coast.

First Settlements

1620 A group of Pilgrims arrives in what is now Massachusetts looking for religious freedom.

1630 Governor John Winthrop from England settles Boston, which becomes the capital of the Massachusetts Bay Colony in 1632.

American Revolution

1773 A growing frustration with British taxes and lack of representation in British government results in a colonial revolt called the Boston Tea Party.

1775 Patriot Paul Revere makes his famous midnight ride to warn the colonists that British troops were marching from Boston to Concord to seize their hidden supply of gunpowder.

The first battles of the American Revolution are fought at Lexington and Concord.

1783 The American Revolution ends in the creation of the United States, with the separation of the American colonies from Great Britain.

New Nation

1788 Massachusetts becomes the sixth state to ratify, or approve, the U.S. Constitution.

1797 John Adams of Massachusetts becomes the second president of the United States, after George Washington.

Early Settlers

The Pilgrims were the first permanent European settlers in Massachusetts. Many of the original settlers came from a small English village called Scrooby. The Pilgrims were a group of **Puritans** who had broken away from the Church of England to form a separate church.

Map of Settlements and Resources in Early Massachusetts

5 Although the soil can be thin, American Indians and the settlers who followed have worked the land to grow crops since the 1600s.

1 The first English settlers in Massachusetts were the Pilgrims. They established Plimouth Plantation.

6 Since the 1550s, American Indians have used cranberries for food, dye, and medicine. By 1650, the English settlers were eating cranberries. Cranberry bogs are located on the South Shore and Cape Cod.

2 Salem was settled by English fishers in 1626. Today it is one of the oldest seaports in New England.

3 English settlers founded Boston in 1630. It became the capital of the Massachusetts Bay Colony in 1632.

4 Since the early settlers first came to the area in 1620, the coastal waters of Massachusetts have always provided a reliable source of seafood.

N

Scale

0   50 Miles

LEGEND

Settlement		Farming	
River		Massachusetts	
Seafood		State Border	
Cranberries			

Some Puritans decided to move to America so they could govern themselves and practice their religion freely. These people later became known as the Pilgrims. In England, they boarded a ship called the *Mayflower*. After a 66-day voyage over rough seas, the ship first landed on November 21 on Cape Cod at what is now Provincetown. Then, on the day after Christmas, it left its 102 passengers nearby at the site of Plymouth. Before landing, 41 of the male passengers signed the Mayflower Compact, which bound the signers to form a government and to follow any laws and rules that might be established.

The first winter at Plymouth was difficult for the Pilgrims. Almost half the settlers died in the harsh conditions. The local Wampanoag tribe was friendly toward the colonists and helped them adjust to their new surroundings. By the autumn of 1621 the Pilgrims had built houses and stored enough food to last through the next winter. The Pilgrims prepared a great feast and were joined by about 90 Wampanoag. This was the beginning of the Thanksgiving Day holiday.

It is said that the Thanksgiving feast shared by the Pilgrims and the Wampanoag lasted for several days.

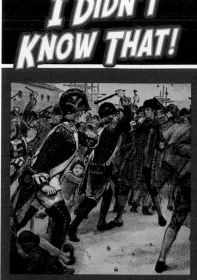

The Boston Massacre occurred on March 5, 1770, when British soldiers clashed with colonists. Bostonians were angry about the Townshend Acts, which placed taxes on many goods. Five colonists died in the conflict, including Crispus Attucks, an African American sailor and former slave. Attucks is considered to be the first person to die in the American Revolution.

Puritans founded America's first **democratic** institution, the town meeting. Every member of the church had the right to speak, and decisions were made by majority rule. Town meetings are still held in New England today.

In 1621 William Bradford was unanimously chosen governor of the Plymouth settlement. He was reelected 30 times.

Notable People

Many people from Massachusetts have contributed to the development of the Bay State as well as their country. Massachusetts has been home to celebrated educators, reformers, and literary figures. It has also provided historic political leaders, from Boston Tea Party organizer Samuel Adams to Deval Patrick, the state's first African American governor, who first took office in 2007.

**JOHN ELIOT
(1604–1690)**

John Eliot, born in England in 1604, came to Boston in 1631. He worked as a Puritan missionary to American Indians in New England. In 1645, Eliot founded the Roxbury Latin School. In 1661, he printed the first Bible in North America. It translated the New Testament into the language of the Massachuset Indians.

**BENJAMIN FRANKLIN
(1706–1790)**

Benjamin Franklin, the brilliant inventor, scientist, statesman, and author, was born in Boston in 1706. He invented bifocal spectacles, the Franklin stove, and swimming fins. His experiments with electricity led to the lightning rod. A political leader in the American Revolution, Franklin helped draft the Declaration of Independence.

DOROTHEA DIX
(1802–1887)

Born in Hampden, which is now in Maine, in 1802, Dix worked as a reformer for the welfare of those with mental illness. She began this work after a trip to a jail where she witnessed harsh treatment of the mentally ill. In 1834, she petitioned the Massachusetts state legislature to build separate hospitals to treat mental illness.

LOUISA MAY ALCOTT
(1832–1888)

Louisa May Alcott, who grew up in Boston and Concord, began writing early in her life. She wrote hundreds of stories, poems, and books. Her best-known work is the autobiographical novel *Little Women*, written in 1868 and 1869. Alcott also worked throughout her life for the abolition of slavery and for voting rights for women.

Robert Goddard (1882–1945) was a scientist and inventor known as the Father of Rocketry. He was a leader in the development of the first liquid-fueled rockets. Born in Worcester, Goddard lived much of his life in Massachusetts.

Rachael Ray (1968–) was born on Cape Cod. The celebrity chef has launched a talk show, writes cookbooks, and publishes her own magazine.

EDWARD KENNEDY
(1932–2009)

Born in Brookline in 1932, Kennedy took office as a U.S. senator from Massachusetts in 1962, a position he held for almost 47 years. His brothers were John F. Kennedy, who served as the 35th U.S. president, and Robert Kennedy, who was a member of his brother's presidential cabinet. Edward Kennedy died in 2009.

Population

Massachusetts has more than 6.5 million residents. The state is divided into 14 counties, and the counties include nearly 50 cities and more than 300 towns. Boston, the state capital, is by far the largest city in the state. It is a major business center and Atlantic seaport. Worcester, with more than 180,000 people, is the second-largest city. Other large Massachusetts cities include Springfield, Cambridge, and Lowell. Located across the Charles River from Boston, Cambridge is a cultural, educational, and business center. The state also has one of the most educated workforces. About one in three people in Massachusetts has at least a bachelor's degree.

Massachusetts Population 1950–2010

The population of Massachusetts has grown in every decade since 1950, but the increase has usually not been large. What factors might make a state's population grow only slowly?

Number of People

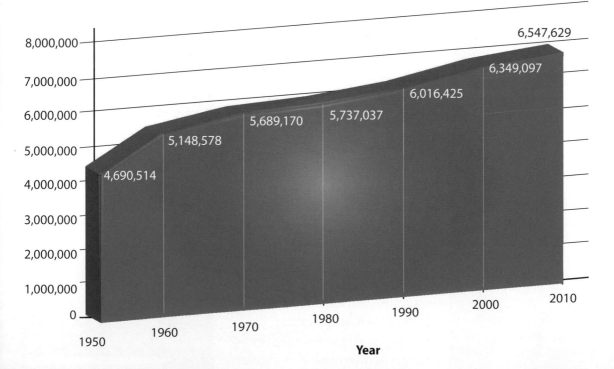

The state's population is mostly urban, with more than 80 percent of the people living in cities or towns.

On December 18, 1990, the state government proclaimed that the residents of Massachusetts would officially be called Bay Staters.

The Bay State is officially known as the Commonwealth of Massachusetts. A commonwealth is a whole body of people that makes up a nation or a state.

Massachusetts is one of the most densely populated states. There are about 835 residents per square mile.

About 6 percent of the population of Massachusetts consists of children under five years old.

Politics and Government

Politics has always been important in Massachusetts. During colonial days, Massachusetts became a center of revolutionary activity. The first battles of the American Revolution were fought at Lexington and Concord in 1775. Massachusetts also led the struggle to outlaw slavery in the 1800s.

Built in 1798, the Massachusetts State House is located across from the Boston Common. The dome was originally made out of wood shingles. Today the dome is copper, covered with 23 karat gold to prevent leaks.

Massachusetts entered the Union on February 6, 1788, becoming the sixth state to ratify, or approve, the new U.S. Constitution. The state's constitution, adopted on October 25, 1780, is the world's oldest constitution still in effect. The state government is led by a governor who is directly elected by the people. The state legislature consists of two houses. They are a 40-member Senate and a 160-member House of Representatives. The highest court in the state is the Supreme Judicial Court.

The state song of Massachusetts is called "All Hail to Massachusetts."

Here is an excerpt from the song:

All hail to Massachusetts,
the land of the free
and the brave!
For Bunker Hill and
Charlestown, and flag we
love to wave;
For Lexington and Concord,
and the shot heard 'round
the world;
All hail to Massachusetts,
we'll keep her flag
unfurled.
She stands upright for
freedom's light that shines
from sea to sea;
All hail to Massachusetts!
Our country 'tis of thee!

The constitution of the Commonwealth of Massachusetts, including a declaration of the rights, was approved in 1780. This document later influenced the drafting of the U.S. Constitution and Bill of Rights.

Cultural Groups

Although American Indians played a prominent role in the early history of Massachusetts, today only about 15,000 American Indians remain in the state. Present-day tribes include the Wampanoag and the Nipmuc. The Massachusetts Center for Native American Awareness helps these people preserve their traditions.

The English were the first Europeans to establish permanent settlements in Massachusetts. English influence is apparent in the buildings, laws, and culture of the state. Some descendants of these early settlers became very rich and formed a kind of upper class in Boston. These prominent families became known as the Brahmins. Descendants of the Puritan settlers governed Massachusetts for more than 200 years.

In the 1800s a wave of **immigration** brought many new settlers to Massachusetts. First came the Irish, who fled the Great Potato Famine in their homeland during the 1840s. Later came Italians, Portuguese, Scandinavians, Poles, and others from Europe. Immigration has fundamentally altered the makeup of the state. Once predominantly Protestant, the state is now largely Roman Catholic.

Many Irish families came to Massachusetts, mostly to Boston, to avoid starvation during the Great Potato Famine in Ireland.

Today Massachusetts draws many immigrants from Asia, Latin America, Africa, and the Caribbean. Hispanic Americans are the largest minority group, making up about 9 percent of the state's total population. African Americans make up 7 percent of the state's population, although the percentage is higher in the Boston area. About 5 percent of the state's residents are of Asian descent.

About one in eight people in Massachusetts was born outside the United States. Many of them immigrated from Spanish-speaking countries. Protecting the rights of immigrants is an important political issue in the state.

In 1960 Americans elected an Irish Bostonian as the country's 35th president. John F. Kennedy was the first Roman Catholic to be elected president.

The Black Heritage Trail explores the history of Boston's African American community of the 1800s. This walking tour encompasses 14 historical sites in Boston's Beacon Hill area.

Massachusetts has more than 300,000 residents of French Canadian descent, more than any other New England state.

The African Meeting House on Boston's Smith Court was built in 1806. It is the oldest standing African American church in the country.

Arts and Entertainment

Massachusetts has a thriving arts and entertainment scene. Boston in particular has always been known as a cultural center for New England and for the United States as a whole.

Throughout its history the Bay State has produced many important writers, artists, and entertainers. Ralph Waldo Emerson, Henry David Thoreau, Nathaniel Hawthorne, Emily Dickinson, Edgar Allan Poe, and John Cheever are among the most famous writers born in the state. Massachusetts has also produced many important painters, such as Albert Pinkham Ryder, who painted mystical and romantic seascapes. Boston native Winslow Homer is also known for painting marine subjects. James Whistler, born in Lowell, is most famous for his painting commonly known as "Whistler's Mother." Television and movie stars from Massachusetts include Bette Davis, Leonard Nimoy, Jay Leno, Matt Damon, and Ben Affleck.

Edgar Allan Poe, author of The Raven and Other Poems, *also wrote some of the first modern detective stories.*

Franklin Park Zoo is home to animals from around the world, including gorillas, white-bearded wildebeests, and Bengal tigers.

Ben Affleck and Matt Damon grew up together in Cambridge. The film *Good Will Hunting* won the team an Academy Award for best screenplay of 1997. Since then, Affleck has starred in dozens of films and directed *Gone Baby Gone* and *The Town*. Damon has also starred in numerous films, including the Bourne movies.

The Boston Ballet, founded in 1963, is now one of the largest dance companies in the United States.

The Peabody Essex Museum, founded in Salem in 1799, is the country's oldest continuously operating museum.

One of the top cultural attractions in Massachusetts is the Boston Symphony Orchestra, or BSO. It was formed in 1881 by Henry Lee Higginson. During the spring season, the BSO performs as the Boston Pops, playing light classics, show tunes, and pop music. The BSO's summer home is the 500-acre Tanglewood Estate, just south of Lenox. The Tanglewood Music Festival features choirs, popular music, and jazz in addition to performances by the BSO.

Throughout the state, but especially in Boston and the other coastal cities and towns, the past is preserved in historic buildings, monuments, museums, and libraries. Other notable attractions include Boston's Franklin Park Zoo and the New England Aquarium.

Sports

S cenic and recreational attractions are numerous in Massachusetts. The chief seaside resort areas are Cape Ann, the north shore between Cape Ann and Boston, Cape Cod, and the offshore islands of Martha's Vineyard and Nantucket. All along the coastline, swimming, boating, and fishing are popular.

Sports have long been a passion for the people of Massachusetts. Boston was one of the first cities in the United States to have professional teams in baseball, basketball, and hockey. The Boston Red Sox are one of America's favorite baseball teams. The team won five World Series between 1903 and 1918 and, after an 86-year wait, captured another championship in 2004. They also won in 2007. The Red Sox play their home games at Fenway Park. This famous ballpark first opened on April 20, 1912, and it is the oldest in the major leagues.

Fenway Park is one of the smallest parks in the big leagues, with a seating capacity of about 37,000 people. It is known for its odd shape, its hand-operated scoreboard, and especially its tall left-field wall known as the Green Monster.

Among the other professional teams in Massachusetts, the Boston Celtics of the National Basketball Association, or NBA, have historically been the most successful. The Celtics have won 17 NBA championships, more than any other team. They dominated the league from 1957 to 1969, when they won 11 NBA championships in 13 years. The team won its 17th title in 2008. The Celtics share their home at TD Garden with hockey's Boston Bruins.

The state's National Football League team, the New England Patriots, plays its games in Foxboro, south of Boston. Originally called the Boston Patriots, the team was one of professional football's finest in the early 21st century, winning Super Bowl titles in 2002, 2004, and 2005. Quarterback Tom Brady has broken records playing for the team since 2000.

The New England Patriots' star quarterback Tom Brady was named Most Valuable Player of the 2010 season.

I DIDN'T KNOW THAT!

Boston brought home the Stanley Cup in 2011 when the Bruins defeated the Vancouver Canucks in game seven of the Stanley Cup Finals. It was Boston's first Stanley Cup Championship since 1972.

The Boston Marathon is the world's oldest annual marathon. It began in 1897 and was inspired by the 1896 Olympic marathon in Athens, Greece.

Boston was the site of the first World Series in 1903. The Red Sox defeated Pittsburgh 5 games to 3.

Heavyweight boxer Rocky Marciano of Brockton was the only world champion who won every fight, 49 in all, when he retired in 1956.

Cambridge's Head of the Charles **Regatta** takes place at the end of October. First held in 1965, it is the largest two-day regatta in the world.

National Averages Comparison

T he United States is a federal republic, consisting of fifty states and the District of Columbia. Alaska and Hawai'i are the only non-contiguous, or non-touching, states in the nation. Today, the United States of America is the third-largest country in the world in population. The United States Census Bureau takes a census, or count of all the people, every ten years. It also regularly collects other kinds of data about the population and the economy. How does Massachusetts compare with the national average?

Comparison Chart

United States 2010 Census Data *	USA	Massachusetts
Admission to Union	NA	Feb. 6, 1788
Land Area (in square miles)	3,537,438.44	7,840.02
Population Total	308,745,538	6,547,629
Population Density (people per square mile)	87.28	835.15
Population Percentage Change (April 1, 2000, to April 1, 2010)	9.7%	3.1%
White Persons (percent)	72.4%	80.4%
Black Persons (percent)	12.6%	6.6%
American Indian and Alaska Native Persons (percent)	0.9%	0.3%
Asian Persons (percent)	4.8%	5.3%
Native Hawaiian and Other Pacific Islander Persons (percent)	0.2%	—
Some Other Race (percent)	6.2%	4.7%
Persons Reporting Two or More Races (percent)	2.9%	2.6%
Persons of Hispanic or Latino Origin (percent)	16.3%	9.6%
Not of Hispanic or Latino Origin (percent)	83.7%	90.4%
Median Household Income	$52,029	$65,304
Percentage of People Age 25 or Over Who Have Graduated from High School	80.4%	84.8%

*All figures are based on the 2010 United States Census, with the exception of the last two items. Percentages may not add to 100 because of rounding.

How to Improve My Community

Strong communities make strong states. Think about what features are important in your community. What do you value? Education? Health? Forests? Safety? Beautiful spaces? Government works to help citizens create ideal living conditions that are fair to all by providing services in communities. Consider what changes you could make in your community. How would they improve your state as a whole? Using this concept web as a guide, write a report that outlines the features you think are most important in your community and what improvements could be made. A strong state needs strong communities.

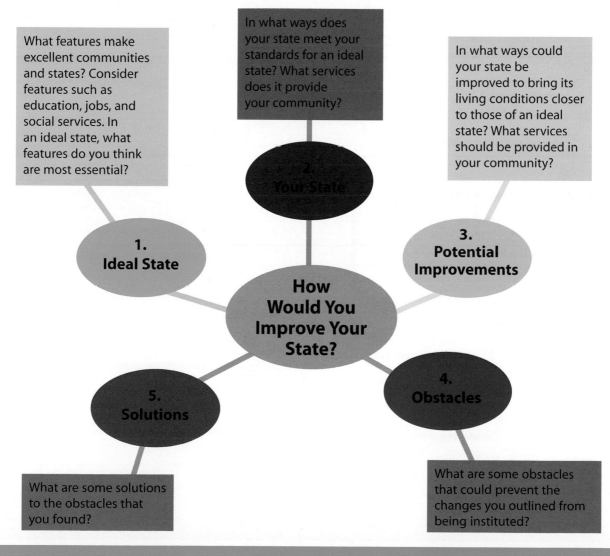

What features make excellent communities and states? Consider features such as education, jobs, and social services. In an ideal state, what features do you think are most essential?

In what ways does your state meet your standards for an ideal state? What services does it provide your community?

In what ways could your state be improved to bring its living conditions closer to those of an ideal state? What services should be provided in your community?

**2.
Your State**

**1.
Ideal State**

**3.
Potential
Improvements**

**How
Would You
Improve Your
State?**

**4.
Obstacles**

**5.
Solutions**

What are some solutions to the obstacles that you found?

What are some obstacles that could prevent the changes you outlined from being instituted?

Exercise Your Mind!

Think about these questions and then use your research skills to find the answers and learn more fascinating facts about Massachusetts. A teacher, librarian, or parent may be able to help you locate the best sources to use in your research.

1 True or False: The Salem witches wore tall pointy hats and flew on broomsticks.

2 What Boston church houses one of the top-ten largest pipe organs in the world?

3 Massachusetts is part of a region called New England. There are six states in New England. What are they?

4 True or False: People in Boston died in a flood of molasses in 1919.

5 What is Plymouth Rock?

6 What Massachusetts city published the first American novel?

7 For what is Springfield native Theodor Geisel famous?

8 True or False: People sipped Earl Grey tea at the Boston Tea Party.

Words to Know

colony: a group of people living in a new place who are under the rule of a parent country

constitution: an official document that sets out basic principles and laws

democratic: relating to a political system in which decisions are made according to the wishes of the majority of people

diverse: made up of different kinds

endangered: in danger of becoming extinct, or completely dying out

extinct: no longer existing

fertile: capable of bearing or producing fruit, vegetation, or crops

habitat: the place where a plant or animal lives and grows

immigration: moving to a new land from another country

industrialized: having developed from an agricultural society to an industrial one

interpreter: someone who translates from one language into another

Nobel laureates: people who are recognized for their achievements by the Nobel Foundation

Puritans: members of a group of Protestants from the Church of England who demanded simpler doctrines and strict religious discipline

regatta: a boat race

revolutionary: producing or characterized by radical change

scribe: a person who copies written documents

textile: cloth or goods produced by weaving, knitting, or felting

whaling: the occupation of catching whales

Index

Log on to www.av2books.com

AV² by Weigl brings you media enhanced books that support active learning. Go to www.av2books.com, and enter the special code found on page 2 of this book. You will gain access to enriched and enhanced content that supplements and complements this book. Content includes video, audio, web links, quizzes, a slide show, and activities.

Audio
Listen to sections of the book read aloud.

Video
Watch informative video clips.

Embedded Weblinks
Gain additional information for research.

Try This!
Complete activities and hands-on experiments.

WHAT'S ONLINE?

Try This!	Embedded Weblinks	Video	EXTRA FEATURES
Test your knowledge of the state in a mapping activity.	Discover more attractions in Massachusetts.	Watch a video introduction to Massachusetts.	**Audio** Listen to sections of the book read aloud.
Find out more about precipitation in your city.	Learn more about the history of the state.	Watch a video about the features of the state.	**Key Words** Study vocabulary, and complete a matching word activity.
Plan what attractions you would like to visit in the state.	Learn the full lyrics of the state song.		
Learn more about the early natural resources of the state.			**Slide Show** View images and captions, and prepare a presentation.
Write a biography about a notable resident of Massachusetts.			
Complete an educational census activity.			**Quizzes** Test your knowledge.

AV² was built to bridge the gap between print and digital. We encourage you to tell us what you like and what you want to see in the future.
Sign up to be an AV² Ambassador at www.av2books.com/ambassador.